I0820057

This book belongs to

________________________

Given with love by

________________________

# St. Martin of Tours

Cover image and design by Angela Glökler
Book design by Lynn Else



Library of Congress Cataloging-in-Publication Data
Names: Hanauer, Michaela author | Glökler, Angela illustrator
Title: St. Martin of Tours: the man who shared his coat / Michaela Hanauer; illustrated by Angela Glökler.
Other titles: Einer, der seinen Mantel teilte....English Saint Martin of tours
Description: New York; Mahwah, NJ: Paulist Press, [2025] | Translation of: Einer, der seinen Mantel teilte...Die Geschichte von Sankt Martin in Bildwörtern. | Audience: Ages 5–9 | Audience: Grades 2–3 | Text in English. Translation from German. | Summary: "This children's book recounts the story of St. Martin of Tours who shared his cloak with a beggar, only to discover the beggar was Christ"—Provided by publisher.
Identifiers: LCCN 2025015917 (print) | LCCN 2025015918 (ebook) | ISBN 9780809168101 paperback | ISBN 9780809189373 ebook
Subjects: LCSH: Martin, Saint, Bishop of Tours, approximately 316–397—Juvenile literature | Christian saints—France—Tours—Juvenile literature | LCGFT: Literature
Classification: LCC BR1720.M3 H26313 2025 (print) | LCC BR1720.M3 (ebook) | DDC 270.2092—dc23/eng/20250807
LC record available at https://lccn.loc.gov/2025015917
LC ebook record available at https://lccn.loc.gov/2025015918

ISBN 978-0-8091-6810-1 (paperback)
ISBN 978-0-8091-8937-3 (ebook)

Published by Paulist Press
997 Macarthur Boulevard
Mahwah, NJ 07430
www.paulistpress.com

Printed and bound in the United States of America
by Versa Press, Inc.
Peoria, Illinois
September 2025

# St. Martin of Tours

## THE MAN WHO SHARED HIS COAT

MICHAELA HANAUER
ILLUSTRATED BY ANGELA GLÖKLER

Paulist Press
New York / Mahwah, NJ

Martin lived a long time ago in the ancient Roman Empire. His father was a soldier and was sent anywhere the emperor needed him. Therefore, Martin and his family moved very often. Nevertheless, he was a cheerful boy and quickly found friends everywhere. Once a friend told him stories about Jesus. Martin was immediately interested. He was thrilled. He wanted to be like Jesus when he grew up!

When he was old enough, Martin would have loved to have become a priest. But at that time, people did not choose what they wanted to do. It was common for boys to become what their fathers were. One father was a farmer, so Martin's friend became a farmer, and one father was a soldier, so the boy had to become a soldier.

That's exactly what Martin's father expected from him. Martin sighed deeply, but then he followed obediently. He learned to ride and became a soldier of the emperor. But Martin also decided to be a helpful soldier and to stay friendly.

Sometimes he even gave his entire salary—this is what you call money—to help people. The other soldiers mocked him. "You will soon starve yourself, while the poor here will eat on golden plates!"

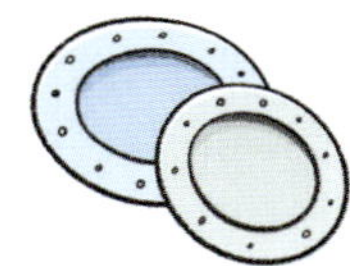

But Martin thought of Jesus and replied with a smile, "Everything that we share, we get back with double the love!"

On a particularly icy winter day, Martin was riding back to town with the other soldiers. Near the wall next to the large gate, someone was crouching. It was a beggar. He only wore a few rags and shivered from the cold.

The other soldiers quickly turned their faces away. They did not want to see or help the suffering beggar. Only Martin felt sorry for him.

But how could he help the beggar? He had already given away his money. And he didn't have anything with him. No bread, no clothes, except for the things he himself was wearing. Martin looked at his armor and his sword. None of this helped against the cold. Except maybe...

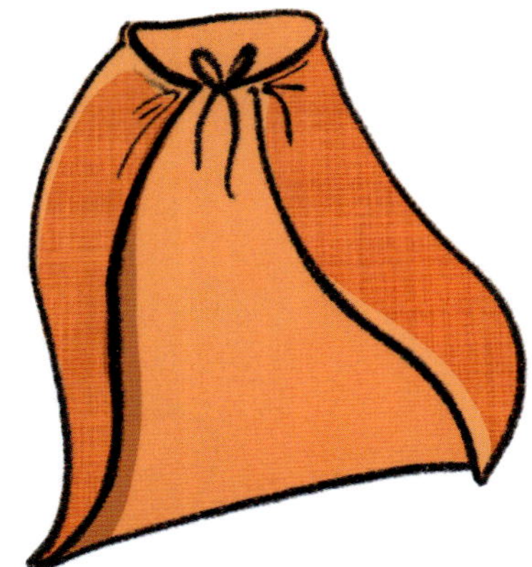

...his big red cloak! That was definitely big enough for two!

Without further ado, he pulled out his sword, took the cloak from his shoulders, and divided it into two halves. He gave one of the halves to the beggar saying, "Please take it! May it warm you as much as it warms me!"

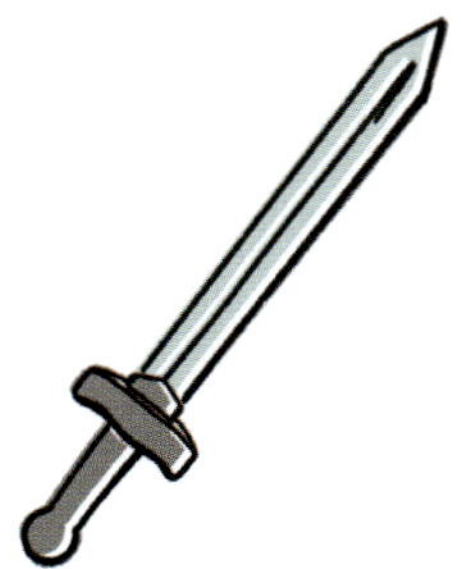

This time the other soldiers laughed at him out loud. But it didn't matter to Martin.

On the following night, Jesus appeared to him in a dream. He was wrapped in half of Martin's cloak, and he thanked Martin saying, "Whatever you did for one of the least of these brothers of mine, you did for me too!"

Martin was overwhelmed and filled with happiness. "From now on I only want to do good things like my hero Jesus!"

Therefore, he decided not to fight against other people. Before the next big battle, he went to the emperor. "Please release me from your service! I can no longer do what you pay me for!"

Outraged, the emperor shouted, "Forget it! You're just a coward!"

"At least allow me to go into battle without a sword and shield, Your Majesty," said Martin.

This the emperor allowed.

When the next morning came, and the battle was supposed to start, an unbelievable thing happened. The opponents surrendered voluntarily! Without any fighting, the Roman soldiers won. Even the emperor saw this as a sign from heaven and was now ready to let Martin go.

Relieved, Martin moved a few miles away from the town. He enjoyed the peace and humbly settled into a small hut. There he prayed a lot and worked hard. He helped all the poor and sick people in the area and had an open ear and an open heart. Word spread about his good deeds and strong faith. After the previous bishop died, he was chosen unanimously to be the new bishop.

But when the priests came to take him to the bishop's palace, he quickly fled into his hut and hid in the darkest corner. They would certainly never have found him, but the geese in the hut excitedly stretched their necks and fluttered their wings and chattered wildly to each other. And so, their noise betrayed the humble Martin.

Covered by white feathers and with bright red cheeks, Martin stood in front of the priests. "If that is God's will, then I will be your bishop. But I am not moving to the bishop's palace. I would rather stay here in my hut!"

His modesty impressed the people as much as his good deeds.

When Martin died, everyone was very sad and cried, the priests as well as the simple farmers. Countless people attended his funeral. Because of the autumn darkness, they carried lanterns in their hands to light the road and find some comfort. Even today, we remember Saint Martin with a lantern parade on November 11!

## ABOUT THE AUTHOR

**Michaela Hanauer** is a Munich native. She studied law and has been a children's and young adult writer for more than fifteen years.

## ABOUT THE ILLUSTRATOR

**Angela Glökler** was born in Rastatt in southern Germany. She studied illustration at the University of Applied Sciences in Hamburg.

PRAYER TO

# St. Martin of Tours

Dear St. Martin,
Like your hero, Jesus, you loved all people,
even your enemies.
You were kind and generous,
and you never turned away from someone who needed help.
Pray for me that I can be strong and loving.
By imitating you, may I learn to follow Jesus
with all my heart and soul.
Amen

# St. Martin

**IS THE PATRON SAINT OF:**

Soldiers

Beggars

Tailors

Wool-weavers

Wine growers

France

Geese

His feast day is November 11.

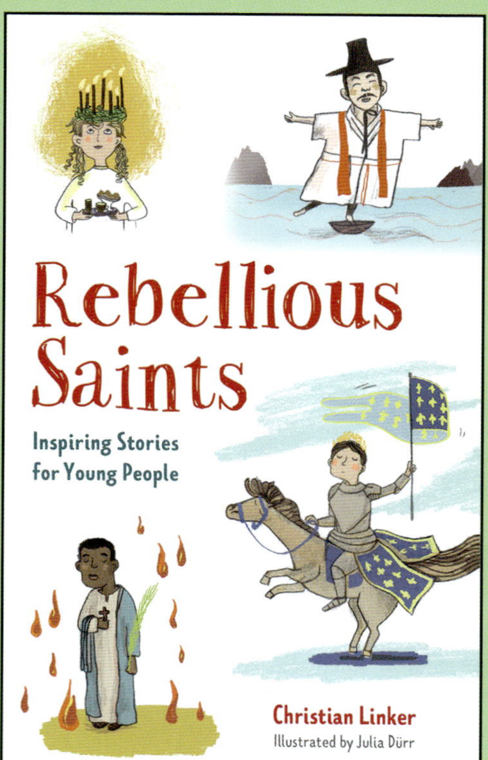


## Rebellious Saints

**Inspiring Stories for Young People**
***Christian Linker***
***Illustrated by Julia Dürr***

Twenty-two saints tell their own exciting story of how they found that desiring God and living for bold truth took them places they never expected to go and empowered them to do remarkable, sometimes very quirky, things.

**Ages 10-12**
**6805-7 $19.95**

# Maximilian Kolbe

**Saint of Auschwitz**
***Elaine Murray Stone***

A middle-grade biography of Maximilian Kolbe, the Polish priest who offered himself at Auschwitz in exchange for the life of a man with two children.

**Ages 8 and up.**
**6637-2 $11.95**

## Elizabeth Ann Seton

**Saint for a New Nation**

***Julie Walters***

A fictionalized young adult biography of Elizabeth Ann Seton (1774–1821), New York socialite, wife, mother, convert, and foundress of the American Sisters of Charity and the first U.S.-born saint.

**Ages 11 and up.**
**6692-5  $12.95**

# The Story of Saint Patrick

***J. Janda***

Prisoner, slave, and saint! Even though a lot of people celebrate the day of the wearing of the green, few know the actual story of this remarkable and exciting man.

**Ages 5-8**
**6623-2 $11.95**